Empowering Persons With Disabilities

A guide to interviewing
persons with disabilities
in stressful situations.

Richard Dicks, Jr.

Manufactured in the United States of America

ISBN: 978-1-886591-27-1

Published for Mr. Dicks by
BLUE CREEK PRESS
Heron, Montana 59844
books@bluecreekpress.com
Editing, proofing and design
provided by Blue Creek Press

Table of Contents

The human spirit
is one of ability,
perseverance and
courage that no
disability can
steal away.

Author unknown

Introduction

It is my responsibility to point out my humble beginnings of working with the intellectually and developmentally disabled population and the overall community of the disabled. My calling as a grade school instructor, Law Enforcement Officer and Child Protective Investigator increased my awareness of developmental capacity and cultural influences when attempting to obtain a truthful and clear narration of events.

The further roles of Civil Rights Investigator/Officer, Section 504/ADA Coordinator, Behavioral Health Clinician and Language Access Coordinator aided in learning to assess cognitive abilities and language skills. These roles and responsibilites have allowed me to understand social and emotional needs and have enhanced my ability to use the narrative process to successfully obtain information and effectively deliver services.

My unique experiences within both public and private agencies offered an opportunity to engage in policy implementation, monitor for compliance and provide training for prevention and re-occurrence, which helps to identify the risks and remedy the effects of abuse and neglect.

The purpose of this guide is to help users become and remain proactive in serving individuals with disabilities affected by crime through public agencies, community-based care organizations and private corporations. Methods of empowerment include offering tips to multidisciplinary teams and collaborating with others in this field.

In this guide, you will find content that will help build a service model. Whether you are working in government, a 501c3 non-profit or a community-based care organization, these tips can help you establish a sound policy. For those working in organizations currently assisting individuals impacted by crime, the stakes could not be higher, and I commend you.

For individuals interested in joining the community, now is the time. The opportunities to provide services to both children and adults with disabilities — and their families — have significantly increased. Likewise, the need for training, patience and appropriate responses that will benefit this community.

By use of this guide, the benefits to victims of crimes against persons with disabilities are potentially enormous. The response will improve their quality of life under appropriate delivery service models and offer a legal aspect to your service.

— Richard Dicks, December, 2020

Credentials of the Author

* Master's Degree in Public Administration with Concentration in Criminal Justice Administration.

* Bachelor's Degree in Management Organization Development

* Graduate of Flint Police Academy

* Graduate of Florida Juvenile Justice Academy

* Graduate of Michigan Department of Corrections Academy

* Certified Court Mediator.

* Service in multiple city, county and state governments as a civil servant in partnership with community and police organizations, as well as working as a behavioral health clinician.

A hero is an ordinary
individual who finds
the strength to
persevere and endure
in spite of
overwhelming
obstacles.

Christopher Reeve

Legal Aspects

Thanks to the Americans with Disabilities Act (ADA) of 1990 and the 2008 ADA amendments, individuals with disabilities are entitled to free service delivery under Title VI of the Civil Rights Act of 1964 and Section 504/ADA of the 1973 Rehabilitation Act.

The entitlement applies to public and private agencies providing services and extends to their contract service providers.

Under ADA, any physical or mental impairment that substantially affects one or more major life activity; has a record of such impairment; or is regarded as having such an impairment is considered a disability.

Examples of major life activities include caring for oneself, performing manual tasks such as walking, seeing, concentrating and interacting with others.

Other examples include sitting, standing, breathing, hearing and lifting; and mental and emotional processes such as speaking, learning and working.

The 2008 ADA amendments include episodic and other physiological impairments such as cognitive, intellectual and developmental disabilities.

The Rehabilitation Act of 1973 intersects with ADA and specifically covers services to those with physical, emotional and sensory disabilities

For the sake of narrowing the scope of this guide, the focus will be on tips for servicing those with sensory, developmental, intellectual, age-related, and cognitive disabilities.

These tips for helping those with disabilities should be incorporated into community partnerships to help lessen the effects of crimes against persons with disabilities.

Deaf and Hard-of-Hearing

The tips and tools presented for dealing with sensory disabilities are universal and shall serve as a model of effective communication with persons who are deaf or hard-of-hearing. In particular, the use of auxiliary aids and services are essential because it allows such persons equal opportunities to participate in and enjoy the benefits of a service, program or activity.

A discussion of auxiliary aids and services is an appropriate step to having a sound policy for the deaf and hard-of-hearing.

Here are some tips:

* Use certified interpreters for sign language access.

* Note taking is an effective way of establishing their preferred method of communication.

7

* Communication Access Real-Time Translation (CART) . This transcription service uses a stenotype machine, computer and real-time software to instantly translate speech into readable text for a seamless captioning experience. A CART provider would be fitting for a group of deaf clients in need of services. This process could be applied for taking depositions, in focus groups, conferences and teleconferences.

* Telephone handset amplifiers, for the hard of hearing

* Telephones compatible with hearing aids closed caption decoders, open and closed captioning.

* Assistive listening devices. i.e., Pocket talkers

* Written materials or note takers should be limited, unless you are a CART provider or are establishing a preferred method of communication

The reason for focusing on auxiliary aids for deaf and hard-of-hearing (DHH) is because private and public sectors of the medical profession, community-based care (CBC), behavioral health clinicians, first responders and frontline employees are more likely to have contact with DHH victims of crime.

Over the years, the deaf community has endured offensive terms and treatment by the general public due to their deafness or hard-of-hearing. For instance, archaic terms such as "deaf and dumb" or "deaf mute" were often used in a manner derogatory to deaf people in the 18th century. That has carried over to the present day. Although the deaf community is largely illiterate to spoken languages by the hearing community, both terms are unacceptable and considered a slur. By beginning with educating professionals first we begin to break the use of archaic terms which are offensive.

Deaf people are born into a world rich with language, but parents may not know that their infant child is deaf. Barring serious neurocognitive impairments, children will have mastered their native language(s) by approximately age 5. The first words are usually spoken by age 1. If deafness of a child is detected between ages 1 and 6, it is known as prelingual deafness. If the deafness of the child occurs between 7 and 9 years of age then it is post-lingual. For a person who becomes deaf as an adult, the term is "deafened."

DDH Children

For DHH children, the acquisition of language, proficiency in whatever language and the experience of gaining access to that language is essential to other developmental domains such as cognition, social-emotional skills, school readiness and academic outcomes.

A deaf child's perceptual inabilities and family language environment, including lack of exposure to sign language, often result in a lack of easily accessible language input for the child. Deprivation of sign language or signing sufficient to support full first language at an appropriate stage impacts the development of the child.

Deaf people impacted at an early age or as adults are led to find their own deaf community to learn from, which affects their literacy rate on both reading and writing. The rate of literacy may also decline for those who are hard-of-hearing.

Categories of Hearing Loss

Loss of hearing has been categorized and includes auditory, conductive, sensorineural and mixed hearing loss.

* Auditory processing disorders occur when the brain has problems processing information contained in sound, such as understanding speech and determining where sounds are coming from.

+ Conductive hearing loss occurs when there is a problem with the outer or middle ear which interferes with passing sound to the inner ear. It can be caused by such things as too much ear wax, ear infections, a punctured eardrum, fluid build-up or abnormal bone growth in the middle ear.

+ Sensorineural hearing loss occurs when the hearing organ —cochlea — and/or the auditory nerve — organ of Corti — are damaged or malfunction, so they are unable to accurately send electrical information to the brain.

The treatment of individuals with disabilities is critical to improving their lives. Hubert Humphrey, speaking on the treatment of those with disabilities, said, "The moral test of government is how that government treats those who are in the dawn of life, the children; those who are in the twilight of life, the elderly; and those who are in the shadows of life, the sick, the needy and the handicapped."

When correctly applied by the professional community and their contracted service providers, these tips will help us pass the test

Tips for Dealing with Deaf or Hard-of-Hearing Victims of Crime

In traumatic situations with individuals who are deaf or hard-of-hearing it is critical to find out their preferred method of communicating. They may need a sign language interpreter, but how does one ask?

* First, establish a short distance between yourself and the individual — 4 to 6 feet — when speaking directly to them.

* Note writing may be helpful to establish their preferred method of communication, but it must be limited to short phrases. "Do you sign in English?" "Do you sign in Creole?" "Do you sign in Spanish?"

* Some deaf people will ask to communicate by notes. Be careful! Note writing and lip reading should not substitute as acceptable communication.

* It is critical to understand that not every deaf individual can read lips. If you attempt lip reading, it must be to establish the deaf individual's preferred method of communications, such as sign language.

+ Avoid raising your voice as an alternative to lip reading.

+ If you choose lip reading, look at the person, speak clearly in short phrases, and slowly enunciate the words in natural progression.

+ Flash cards with words, phrases, objects or drawing of essential needs such as food or water are better.

+ Rudimentary styles of communication such as lip reading and note writing to ask questions should be used only to determine what their preferred method of communication will be in order to provide the correct service. Be prepared to repeat yourself.

In response to a traumatic event, deaf people may express themselves with gestures and movements that seem agitated or aggressive. This may be their interest in getting help.

+ For the individual and the service provider it is critical to use appropriate auxiliary aids and services. The purpose of a certified interpreter is to ensure victims that are deaf or hard-of-hearing receive the appropriate information for services.

Empowering People With Disablities

- Victims who are deaf or hard-of-hearing may want their child or another person under 18 to communicate for them because of personal relationships. Respectfully decline that request and get a certified interpreter for them and you. If that family member or friend misinterprets what occurred, it is more likely that information will impact outcomes.

- Should a deaf individual ask the provider to use a personal friend or relative over age 18, it is permissible, but they should only be used to establish the individual's preferred method of communication and biographical and demographic information.

- In some instances, a provider can use Video Remote Interpreting (VRI) which benefits the victim with disabilities at the point of contact. A VRI interpreter is available within minutes for scheduled virtual visits and within two hours for unscheduled visits. The interaction and interpretation may occur via smart phone, desktop or laptop computer. All are highly desirable interpersonal options to provide immediate language support. The meeting occurs between the deaf individual, the service provider, and certified interpreter in a private setting.

✦ Another method of communicating with individuals with disabilities is Video Relay. (A search for video relay interpreters will lead to different vendors.) The individual with disabilities initiates contact with a video relay operator, and that operator will call a land line or cell phone to establish contact between all parties.

Tips for Using a Video Relay System

✦ If a Video Relay (VR) system is the choice, it is critical to wait for the VR operator to introduce themselves with their operator ID. Such an exchange may occur in this manner: "Hello, this is Video Relay Operator 73285, and I have Dennis on the line." The service provider may want to ask the VR operator to repeat their ID number if they did not catch it the first time, and then speak directly to Dennis about his concern(s).

✦ The VR operator serves as the intermediary for the service provider and deaf person. The process allows all parties to participate to help the deaf person.

✦ Actively listen to the victim with disabilities, refer to them by name when speaking and don't interrupt the operator or deaf person.

✦ If it appears that an overall agreement will not be reached, attempt to find a point of agreement and ask the victim if they would like you to refer them to someone who can better help them. Ask if there is anything else you can do for them.

Tips for Using a Certified Interpreter in Person

✦ If an interpreter is contacted, make sure they are certified and registered with the National Registry of Interpreters for the Deaf by searching rid.org for identification.

✦ If the interpreter's ID is unavailable on rid.org, you may want to ask if the interpreter has a block on their home address which may prevent their ID from being found. If they are not listed on rid.org, the interpreter is less likely to be certified and should not be used.

✦ A service provider may be tempted to use a co-worker who has taken minimal sign language classes. This is risky and prohibited if this will be substituted for using a certified interpreter.

✦ In cases of maltreatment, time is of the essence and auxiliary aids and services must be delivered quickly, which means one must ensure an appropriate accommodation is available for the encounter.

+ In some cases, deaf individuals wear hearing aids but are still unable to hear clearly. If you observe a hearing aid it may be to enable them to accentuate tones or pitches when others speak. Do not assume they can hear in detail.

+ There are times when more than one member of a family with disabilities become victims of crime. If appropriate services are in place, then one may use a CART provider.

+ For the hard-of-hearing, one may use assistive listening devices, which can serve up to 20 persons in a class setting. They come with neck-loops and ADA plaques. Another is a Pocket Talker, or Frequency Modulation (FM) Systems.

+ An Assistive Listening Device (ALD) may be used with Cochlear implants or hearing aids to help a wearer hear sounds and tones.

+ If a certified interpreter or an ALD is not available, reschedule the services to accommodate the individual who is deaf.

Exercise 1: A deaf individual with limited experience using sign language visits a service provider. The service provider has one year of high school in Sign Language interpreting for the deaf. Which of the following should the service provider do?

⏴ *A)*   Interpret to help find out what services the provider can offer.

⏴ *B)*   Take notes and watch the deaf individual's facial expression to see if they understand.

⏴ *C)*   Take notes and write down short phrases to determine the deaf individual's preferred method of communication.

If you chose **C,** you are taking the right steps to help deaf or hard-of-hearing victims of crime with disabilities to get the services they need.

Exercise 2: An interpreting vendor is contacted, and the agency sends an interpreter within an hour. The service provider is excited about the quick arrival because it is an unexpected appointment. The deaf individual begins signing and the interpreter signs back. After a few minutes, the deaf person begins looking frustrated. Which of the following should the service provider do?

◄ *A)* Allow the interpreter to continue and explain to the deaf individual that the interpreter is from a credible agency.

◄ *B)* Ask the interpreter for their Identification number for RID and immediately stop the session, and ask the deaf individual if they understand, then call the vendor.

◄ *C)* Document what occurred and reschedule the services.

If you selected *B* and *C*, you are correct. It is important to ask the interpreter before the services begin. If you forget, it's okay to request their ID at any time. They may not be certified. Check rid.org and call the vendor to report what occurred, then document it.

Incidents like these are impactful to victims with disabilities and must not be minimized. Apologize and communicate in short phrases. Ask if they would like another interpreter. If so, contact another vendor. You may have to ask the client to reschedule.

Scenario: A Child Protective Service (CPS) worker is investigating an allegation of child abuse. The alleged perpetrator is the mother, who is deaf. The victim is her child, who is deaf as well. The CPS worker visited the home without a certified interpreter.

The CPS worker decided to interview the mother without a certified interpreter using hand-written notes. The interview lasted for hours.

Although the CPS worker did not interview the child, he concluded the child had been abused and obtained support from his CPS supervisor for removal. The child became tearful and loud during separation. This continued in three different foster homes.

The mother contacted an advocacy group, which provided an attorney to address the investigation, particularly the hand-written notes.

A court hearing ensued. The court provided its own certified interpreter and determined that the mother's account conflicted with the CPS worker's notes and did not amount to abuse.

The court ordered CPS to locate the child and bring him to court. The mishandling of the case led to a delay due to the number of homes the child had been taken to. The court was furious because of the trauma to the child. This scenario led advocates to push for policy changes.

Here are some of the changes that the agency was required to make:

* Establish a Request for Services/Waiver Form. This includes the name of the deaf person, the type of auxiliary aids, services requested, and the decision to decline or accept of service.

* Create a form for Communication Assistance to ensure documentation outlining the deaf's access to their preferred method of communication, the type of auxiliary aid provided, (for instance, assistive listening device, certified interpreter, note taker, CART provider, etc.), and their disability, i.e., deaf, hard-of-hearing, low vision or blind.

* Create a survey form to be given to the deaf individual to indicate their level of satisfaction with the services. This would be included in the audit. This form would be mailed by the deaf individual to the governing body.

This service delivery model used allows for self-reporting and could work in a number of fields if the tips within this guide are applied.

The only thing
worse than being
blind is having
sight but no vision.

Helen Keller

Visually Impaired

Many of the same tips and processes apply for visually impaired persons. However, here are tips unique to providing services to individuals who are blind or have low vision.

✦ Ensure the individual with a visual impairment knows your name and agency and that the service provider documents the services requested.

✦ Be aware that an increase in other senses is common in those with visual impairment. It is crucial to not speak loudly, but with a normal voice; this will help the process flow much better. Use your speech, assistive technology and a careful choice of words to indicate concern for their well-being, and to remain engaged throughout the process.

Empowering People With Disablities

* Avoid touching or trying to physically assist a blind/low vision person without asking their permission. It is better to ask if they would like you to escort them to the area of service. If so, extend your arm, hand, or elbow.

* If it is necessary for an individual to move to an object such as a desk, tell them it is X steps away to their left, right, front or rear or by clock hours, with 12 o'clock being directly in front of them. *Example:* "The chair is five steps behind you at 4 o'clock."

* Often individuals who are blind or partially sighted have service dogs to accommodate their disability. It is extremely important not to engage the animal as though it is a pet. Never touch the animal.

* When escorting a visually impaired person, give prompts about where you are going, what the next door leads to or what the area you will be entering contains.

* Since the blind or partially sighted person came for services, ask if they read braille and be prepared to offer adjusted writing guides for blind or low vision. The writing guide can be adjusted to the desired width by sliding the right margin guide from side to side. Its built-in notches along

the upper track hold the margin guide in place. It measures 9-3/8 x 1-1/2 and weighs 1.6 oz. The writing guide could be used for a number of writing needs where guidance may be required.

+ The guide is a perfect tool to use when one offers to fill out the forms for them. Explain each document and why the form is legally required by ADA and Section 504.

+ It is critical to follow the policy of your agency by documenting the initial contact, demeanor of the client, and the content of your conversation. This is helpful in establishing what occurred without relying solely on your interpretation.

+ Another tool to help persons who are visually impaired would be transcriptionist. All documents and communication should be transcribed and one must make an effort to provide a transcript of what was discussed. This is a form of scribe assistance.

+ A scribe assistant could be another individual in the office to help you complete the paperwork.

+ Avoid lapses of conversation during the interview and inform the client if you are going to be silent for a time.

No disability or dictionary out there is capable of clearly defining who we are as a person. It's only when we step out of that labeled box that our abilities begin to be fully recognized, giving us a better definition of who we truly are as individuals.

Robert M Hensel

Intellectual and Developmental Disabilities

My experience as a Behavioral Health Clinician includes conducting forensic interviews with children with disabilities who are victims of crime. In some cases, the disabilities were intellectual, developmental and emotional. In such cases, I did not find a universal standard to address disorders such as Asperger's Syndrome, autism, Prader-Will syndrome, cerebral palsy or physical learning, language and other behavioral areas.

Here are some tips to remember when helping persons with intellectual or developmental disabilities:

✦ Eye contact is the most important aspect of communication.

✦ Get as much information as possible in the early stages of the conversation.

✦ Assess the personality of the individual and use those strengths to build a rapport.

Other tips include:

✦ Engage parents, step-parents and other family members as well as case workers and service providers that may be familiar with their behavior.

✦ If possible, find out what a child was told or how they are reacting prior to the interview.

✦ It is important to set the room with adequate space between you and the victim. If limited space becomes the proverbial elephant in the room, it may contribute to lack of information.

✦ The interview should occur in a neutral environment whenever possible. It is not always possible, but a child-friendly environment free from distractions is best.

✦ Interviews should be audio/video-recorded by a behavioral health clinician or other trained personnel.

✦ The conversation should be easy and based on forensic interviewing techniques to obtain a disclosure.

+ Use simple language, not babble or baby talk. It is unintelligible for court proceedings.

+ A person with a developmental disability can be impacted by low density lighting. A well-lighted room is recommended.

+ Find out if there are other disabilities.

In the interest of helping victims with disabilities, the initial interview should occur as close in time to the event or incident in question.

Begin the interview by developing a rapport. Introduce yourself, starting with your first name, and tell them what you do for a living. It may help to tell them that you talk to kids and teenagers for a living.

+ Ask if they can spell their name, when their birthday is and what they did for their birthday.

+ Ask if they know their colors. Use a box of crayons to see if they can identify colors.

+ Ask the victim to describe their room.

+ Customize your vocabulary and statements to the development level of the child. Be patient, comfortable, quiet and calm .

✦ Tell them you have heard everything; there is nothing they can say that you have not heard.

✦ Ask the individual what they did when they woke up that morning. Tell them you want to know everything and not to leave anything out. This line of questioning sets the stage for sequence interviewing. The hour-glass approach will narrow the questions down to a discussion of the reason why they are there to see you.

✦ Use therapy animals to reduce stress; for instance a trained, certified and evaluated facility dog. Therapy animals can also be an entry into the interviewing process.

✦ Be friendly and respectful and listen while the victim speaks. Follow up with questions or comments such as:
"How come you said 'this?'"
"Tell me more about that?"
"You mentioned this happened once. Was that the first time?"
"Was there a second time?"
"Are there any other times this happened?"

✦ Let the child set the pace for the interview. Be

open-minded and consider all explanations. It is easier to adjust by following up with questions.

+ Make sure the victim understands what you are asking. Examples are, "Did (NAME) touch you?" "Did (NAME) touch you on top of your clothes, bottom of your clothes or inside your clothes?"

+ Some questions may require a visual aid like a box of crayons. Take a crayon out and ask the victim if the crayon is on top, bottom, side, or inside the box.

+ If you need to repeat questions, wait to ask them later.

+ Never use phrases like, "Did (NAME) hurt you?" You may want to say, "How did (NAME) touch you?" Language matters.

+ It is extremely important not to interrupt the victim during the interview. If there is a need to follow up, it is helpful to use books, drawings, crayons, or pictures to elicit information.

+ Use even tones and remain relaxed during the conversation, then follow up with open ended questions. It is critical to use time management as well.

* If the victim becomes tearful, offer some Kleen-ex and ask if they would like to take a break. It might be a good time to ask if it is okay for you to take a bathroom break.

* Some victims may not realize they are victims. This may require a different line of questioning. For instance,
"How did you meet?"
"What kinds of things do you like to do?"
"What do you do together?"

* If the interview becomes uncomfortable, persons with intellectual and developmental disabilities may get up and move around in the room. The movement is cues about their comfortability. It may or may not be because of what you are asking.

* If it appears that you may have come close to the information needed and the child deviates from the topic, engage in ongoing conversation and listen. You may be anxious to get back on track, but the child's statements could lead you back to the topic. Be patient!

* Use non-threatening demeanor and reassure the victim that you are there to keep them safe.

✦ A single interviewer is preferable, because it will minimize the child's distress. However, the process requires sharing information obtained. When possible, coordinate with law enforcement, investigators, and other fact finders.

✦ Agencies should implement or extend streamlined interviewing and intake procedures so that victims with disabilities, particularly those with cognitive or communications disabilities, do not have to bear repeated interviews in different locations.

✦ For victims with autism, be aware of comfortable distance.

✦ Some individuals with disorders require a speech therapist in the interview. Agencies should be prepared to provide an individual familiar with a victim's speech pattern.

✦ The interview will require report writing but it is critical to capture the interview with video and audio recordings under the doctrine of ChildFirst. Assure the recording equipment is functioning correctly. I once interviewed a child and obtained a disclosure, but the equipment malfunctioned and that became the epicenter of the court proceeding.

Ageing is just
another word
for living.

Cindy Joseph

Elderly and Aged Victims with Disabilities

The world's population continue to age, and the elderly are more likely to have disabilities and be victims of crime. The most vulnerable are likely to live alone, live in high crime neighborhoods and rely on walking or public transportation. Following are tips that will reduce the trauma.

+ Assess the person for barriers of fear before approaching by learning about previous trauma and any mood-altering medications. Recognize that some fear is healthy.

+ Take time to introduce yourself and be patient in asking the elderly to respond. If the victim is agitated allow them to time to deescalate.

Empowering People With Disablities

* Start by talking about others, such as asking about ancestors.

* Transition to childhood memories. Use family photos if possible.

* Make an effort not to overdo a discussion of family matters.

* Avoid discussing what happened to them if the individual appears disoriented. Ask them if they are okay and respond accordingly.

* When interviewing the elderly, be prepared to repeat questions.

* Ask yes or no questions.

* Stay clear of talk about placements into facilities. This may create a fear of losing their independence.

* Use plain language and be brief while discussing the crime against them. Let them lead.

* Take breaks from interviewing elderly victims. It will help them to process information.

- Contact family members or neighbors who may offer assistance in narrowing down a list of offenders.

- Make every effort to record the interview because the elderly may not want to repeat.

> If there is one thing I've learned in my years on this planet, it is that the happiest and most fulfilled people are those who devoted themselves to something bigger and more profound than merely their own self-interest.
>
> *John Glenn*

The reality that the
(intellectually disabled)
person is a version of
myself is one from
which so much can be
learned and gained,
and yet, it is a reality
which most people
deny and try to
escape from.

Wolf Wolfensberger

Cognitive Disabilities

Victims with cognitive disabilities may be affected in their judgement, reasoning, perception, awareness and learning ability due to trauma. However, the mental processes of such an individual should not be confused with ineptitude or stupidity. Cognitive disorders affect the brain and audio processing. It is important to develop a list of individuals with experience interviewing individuals with cognitive disabilities. This provides interviewers with a structured approach to help remember specific details.

Be aware of different types of cognitive disabilities such as dyslexia, genetic disabilities, brain injury, Attention Deficit Hyperactivity Disorder (ADHD) and learning disorders.

+ Introductions are effective when interviewing victims with cognitive disabilities.

+ Forensic Experimental Trauma Interviewing (FETI) may be the best approach. This science-informed interviewing framework addresses high stress and trauma on the brain, influences the practice for information collection and accurately documents the interviewee's experience in a neutral, equitable and fair manner.

+ Reduce distractions and create a warm atmosphere

+ Victims with cognitive disabilities may be easily influenced or eager to please you.

+ Avoid asking leading questions, "You were in Las Vegas last week, weren't you?" It is better to ask short, open-ended questions such as, "How exactly did the fight between the two of you occur?"

+ Never ask compound questions, such as, "Did you look down and then look up before you were hit?"

+ Take time to develop a rapport. Ask them to describe who you are. Give them time to answer.

+ Stay away from phrases like, "You have a disability" or "You have dementia."

+ Be patient and ask single questions. For instance, "Did you drink today?" Let them respond to your question. Use plain language and make sure your speech matches theirs.

+ Ensure that you use lots of eye contact throughout the interview.

+ Use non-verbal cues/signals like hand gestures to direct them when giving instructions.

+ It is vital to ask persons with Alzheimer's to describe words they are using to get an understanding of what they mean by them.

+ Enlist a victim's family members or care providers to help work with individuals with cognitive disabilities.

+ At times when the individual may be confused, avoid using a baby talk or demeaning words because it may offend them. Their dignity is one of the few things they have left.

* When communicating in groups include individuals with cognitive disabilities in the conversation.

* Avoid arguing, conflict, or creating stressful situations. It will arouse fear and agitation.

* There is little benefit in conducting extra interviews. Emphasis should be placed on the answers to original questions.

> Our real disabilities
> come from inside us;
> don't tell yourself you
> can't do something.
> Keep trying and if one
> way doesn't work,
> try another.
>
> *Rashida Rowe*

Community Partnerships and Victims with Disabilities

In the context of helping victims of crime with disabilities, it is my intent to reach collaborative partnerships. The formation of partnerships will depend on the types of services needed and available. In most formal settings, there is potential harm when services overlap one another. Moreover, to improve response to victims of crime with disabilities, these partnerships must include community members who have the authority to make changes with their agencies.

Currently there are multidisciplinary teams who assess problems as a whole. There is no need for a monolithic team because the disabled community is comprised of many smaller communities that vary from one geographic location to another, and according to the type of disability.

Consequently, not all advocates support mandatory reporting of crimes against people with disabilities. Individual agencies, organizations or non-profits struggling to maintain independence may perceive mandated reporting as excessive. Others believe that reporting crimes against vulnerable adults is fundamental to ensuring their safety.

Highlighting best practices is pertinent to empowering victims of crime with disabilities through public and private partnership for training, effective programs, and supportive viable alternatives to victim assistance.

Barriers for victims with disabilities have been significantly reduced, but the reporting process in an environment that has become increasingly hostile may reduce reporting by those with disabilities. A systematic approach to elicit information and use of specialized equipment or auxiliary aids for service delivery will produce results.

> The only disability in life is a bad attitude
>
> *Unknown*

Conclusion

The purpose of this guide is to help empower victims of crime with disabilities and improve a systematic approach to service delivery for public, private, and community-based corporations.

We must keep the disabled community in mind during these delicate times. In addition to providing tips for policy implementation, a way to examine the collective effort would be to monitor.

As advocates we can be concerned and supportive without using stigmatizing words to address the disabled community. The word "victim" imposes a negative social identity when used in conjunction with disability. Although the term was frequently used throughout this guide, it is preferable to use "survivor" because that appropriately describes their status in the aftermath of violent or repeated victimization.

This guide is also provided to encourage networking and cross-training in all stages of policy development, decision-making, program development, and service delivery for survivors of crime with disabilities. As such, qualified persons with disabilities should be recruited to help train volunteers, paid staff members and other representatives within the framework of community partnership.

> For too long, the victims of crime have been forgotten persons of our criminal justice system. Rarely do we give victims the help they need or the attention they deserve. Yet the protection of our citizens — to guard them from becoming victims — is the primary purpose of our penal laws. Thus, each new victim personally represents an instance in which our system has failed to prevent crime. Lack of concern compounds that failure.
>
> *President Ronald W. Reagan in the Proclamation declaring the First National Crime Victims Rights Week — April 1, 1981*

Resources

There are varied resources for victims with disabilities. This list provides technical assistance for services, technical referral, or outreach to address issues within the disability community.

+ U.S. Department of Justice 800-514-0301

+ U.S. Equal Employment Opportunity Commission
. 800-669-3362

+ Autism Speaks 888-288-4762

+ Race, Abuse, & Incest National Network (RANN)
. 800-656-4673

+ Disability Rights and Resources. . . . .
. . . . www.disability.gov

+ Registry of Interpretation of the Deaf. . . . .
. . . . .info@rid.org   571-257-3957

+ U.S. Health & Human Services . . . .
. . . . .OCRComplaints@hhs.gov

+ National Center for Victims of Crime . . . .
. 202-467-8700

+ National Organization on Disability. . . . .
. 646-505-1191

Empowering People With Disablities

- United Cerebral Palsy 800-872-5287
- National Center for Learning Disabilities . . . .
  . . . . .www.NCLD.org
- American Sign Language Network 206-527-9555
- Violence against People with Disabilities . . . . .
 951-688-5141
- National Association of Councils of Developmental Disabilities 202-506-5813
- National Alliance on Mental Illness. . . . .
  800-950-6264
- U.S. Dept of Labor Job Accommodation Network
 800-526-7234

Acknowledgments

In preparation of writing this guide, I sought guidance from various sources. First, I give thanks to the one true Source, Substance, Limits, and Bounds of all Creation, Yahweh Elohim through His Son Yahshua. I acknowledge the Creator who is in me for inspiring the creation of this guide for assisting the vulnerable. I am grateful to Him for bringing all things pertaining to my experiences in this area — whatever they may be. — and for inspiring these suggestions for helping victims of crimes against persons with disabilities.

Second, I am grateful to my wife Patricia for her encouragement, unwavering love and patience throughout several projects I have endeavored to complete. Patty, you are extraordinary. This guide could not have been completed without your tolerance of me waking you up in the middle of the morning to discuss ideas for this project and others. Thank you for your emotional support and feedback.

Although I would like to lean on my training, skills, and abilities that, in part, inspired me to take the necessary steps, I am thankful to Roger Robinson, who continues to be instrumental in shaping the field in service delivery.

I cannot forget Stacy Bromfield and Jamny Coronado, whom I declare forensic interviewing experts that can help any organization or special victims' unit achieve their goals. Thank you for your guidance.

Thanks, as well, to Sandy Compton and Blue Creek Press for all of their good work on assisting with the production of this booklet.

Last, I would be remiss if I did not thank my mentor, friend and former manager, Dick Valentine. Dick, you made a special trip to my assigned region specifically to spend the day with me. Your time and attention continued in my early years of service and they shaped my career, as well as my understanding about facilitating, collecting and coordinating service delivery models. You inspire me to give everything I have and leave nothing undone in the field of service.

Thank you!